JUGGLING
is for me

Nancy Marie Temple
and Rande Aronson

photographs by
Bob and Diane Wolfe

Lerner Publications Company   Minneapolis

The authors wish to thank Kari Johnson and Nathan Kokernot—two young jugglers—as well as Wayne and Jean Johnson and Mary Kokernot for all of their help and cooperation. They also extend a special thanks to Keith Johnson; the Matthews Community Center staff; the staff and management of the Minnesota Renaissance Festival in Shakopee, Minnesota; and everyone else who helped to make this book possible.

Photographs on pages 22, 23, 24, and 25 (top, left and right) by Lois Conmy. Cover photograph by Wayne R. Johnson.

For Marie Pfeil Temple — N.M.T.

To Lila and Len — R.A.

LIBRARY OF CONGRESS CATALOGING IN PUBLICATION DATA

Temple, Nancy Marie.
  Juggling is for me.

  (A Sports for me book)
  Summary: Young people explain the history and demonstrate the techniques of juggling.
  1. Jugglers and juggling—juvenile literature.
  [1. Jugglers and juggling] I. Aronson, Rande.
  II. Wolfe, Robert L., ill. III. Wolfe, Diane, ill.
  IV. Title. V. Series: Sports for me books.
  GV1559.T46   1986   793.8   85-23792
  ISBN 0-8225-1146-0 (lib. bdg.)

Manufactured in the United States of America

International Standard Book Number: 0-8225-1146-0
Library of Congress Catalog Card Number: 85-23792

1 2 3 4 5 6 7 8 9 10 95 94 93 92 91 90 89 88 87 86

Hi! My name is Nathan, and this is my friend Kari. We have been learning a lot about juggling lately, and we'd like to tell you about it. I taught myself to juggle two years ago. It was really exciting when my three tennis balls stayed up for the first time!

3

Kari got interested in juggling this summer when her new neighbor Rande moved in. Rande is a professional juggler. When Kari first saw him, he was preparing his act for an upcoming Renaissance festival. Kari was amazed by Rande's juggling skills.

Sometimes Rande juggled **balls**. He also juggled **clubs**, or pins, and sometimes he even juggled **spirit sticks**. For his Renaissance act, Rande also practiced speaking in rhyme while he juggled. He called this talk his "**patter**."

One day, Kari invited me over to meet
Rande. I could hardly believe my eyes when
I saw him juggle! I could see that I had a
lot more to learn, and Rande agreed to help
us both become better jugglers.

Rande told us that juggling is the art of keeping objects in motion in the air by tossing them up and catching them. He said that various forms of juggling had been practiced in ancient Egyptian, Roman, and Chinese cultures. Wall paintings of jugglers that may date from 1900 B.C. have been found in tombs near the Nile River in Egypt. There are also records of early juggling in India, Mexico, and North America.

Rande said that for many hundreds of years in Europe, knowing how to juggle was a rare skill. Then in the 1600s during the Renaissance, juggling was brought back, or revived, by jesters and court jugglers. In the years that followed, only a few people mastered the art, and most of them were performers with traveling circuses.

Today, people of all ages are discovering that juggling is not only fascinating to watch but also a lot of fun to do. Rande told us that more and more people are learning how to juggle, and the sport is now spreading from the circus spotlight to living rooms, parks, and neighborhood centers.

Juggling can be learned with very little equipment. Only three balls are needed for **ball juggling**. The balls should be heavy enough for their weight to be felt when they are caught, and each ball should fit in the hand comfortably so that the fingers are able to close part way around it.

Beginners often start with tennis balls filled with water, dog balls (found in most pet shops), or small **beanbags**, which bounce and roll less than balls. If they aren't too large for a young juggler to handle, hard rubber **lacrosse balls** are even better juggling objects because of their size, weight, and amount of bounce.

Rande said a grassy area outside is a good place for learning how to juggle because the grass helps to bring a rolling ball to a quick halt. If you are learning to juggle indoors, move aside extra furniture, lamps, and other breakable items. To help control falling balls and reduce your chasing a bit, you may want to try juggling over a couch or a bed.

Juggling is not as mysterious and difficult as it may look. By using a step-by-step approach and with concentration and practice, almost anyone can learn to juggle in the crisscross pattern known as the **three-ball cascade**.

An easy way to learn the three-ball cascade is to first practice with scarves. Rande taught Kari **scarf juggling** in about five minutes. Starting with two scarves in the right hand and one in the left, he released them *diagonally* in front of himself: first a right, then the left, then the second right. Since scarves are lightweight, they float downward slowly.

Next, Rande showed Kari the steps that lead to three-ball juggling. First, he told her to stand with her elbows at her sides, to bend her arms, and to hold her upturned, cupped hands at waist level. He asked her to imagine that her hands were holding the lower corners of a rectangular frame that reached just above her head. Rande called the space within this frame the "**working space**" because the "work"—the movement of the hands and the objects being juggled—should be within the frame.

Rande placed one ball in Kari's right hand and asked her to toss the ball up to just above the height of her head—or a little higher—since the higher the ball is thrown, the more time you'll have to catch it. The ball should travel in an arc toward the *opposite* corner of the frame and should reach its highest point, or peak, in the left side of the frame. Rande told Kari to keep her eyes looking straight out at the peak point while she caught the ball with her left hand because there would not be time to be looking up and down when juggling three balls.

Then Rande told Kari to toss the ball
from her left hand to her right. Again, he
had her try to peak the ball at just above
her head, but this time in the *right* side of
the frame. While Kari practiced this one-
ball exchange, Rande reminded her to keep
her elbows at her sides and to try to keep
her hands and the ball within the frame.

After Kari was able to exchange one ball smoothly, Rande asked me to demonstrate the **two-ball exchange**. I started with two balls, one cupped in each hand, and tossed the right ball upward. Then, just as it rounded the peak point and started to drop, I tossed up the left ball. My left hand was then free to catch the first ball coming down.

I continued in this crossover pattern while Kari tried it. Rande told her to try to toss the right and the left balls with the *same* force so that they reached about the same height. After quite a few drops, Kari started to exchange the two balls back and forth. Rande said it would be best to practice this move over and over until it began to feel easy and natural.

At first, Rande stressed, beginners will miss and drop many balls. He said to expect this and, when it happened, to simply pick up the dropped ball, relax, and try again. The drops are part of learning and don't mean that one is not cut out to be a juggler. When learning a new trick, even experienced jugglers drop and chase many balls. Rande told us to think of our drops as "quick breaks" and a way to relax and stretch our muscles by moving in different directions.

Next, Rande showed Kari how to "experience" three-ball juggling by using a **juggling simulation**. In a simulation, someone acts as a "helper" and moves the balls from their peak points to the beginner's waiting hands. Start with two balls in the right hand and one in the left. First, toss up the outer right ball and then the left, just as in the two-ball exchange. Now, without missing a beat, throw up the second right-hand ball while your helper places the first ball in your left hand. Then the helper will place the left ball in your right hand. Continue this pattern with a steady, even beat.

Now Kari was ready to try the cascade on her own. At first, she kept dropping a ball after the second throw. Rande said she was pausing a little too long before the third throw. He suggested she count out loud in an even rhythm—"1, 2, 3, 1, 2, 3"—and try to throw *on* the count. She practiced and practiced. Two days later, she was juggling!

For the next few weeks, Kari and I had fun practicing together. Rande helped us learn to control the cascade, sometimes making it larger and slower, sometimes smaller and faster. Rande was also busy with the final preparations for his juggling act. We helped him check over and pack his costume and props.

Finally, the opening day of the Renaissance festival arrived. Kari and I rode to the festival with Kari's older sister. When we got there, we first checked the printed program for the times and locations of Rande's juggling acts. On our way to his first performance, we passed all sorts of musical and sporting events, booths with freshly baked bread and other treats, displays of handcrafted items, and hundreds of people in colorful costumes. We saw dancers, face painting—and even the king and queen of the festival!

Rande's first performance was at a small open theater called the "Gypsy Stage." Seeing his complete act was even more exciting than we had expected it to be. The audience liked Rande's funny rhymes, and they laughed and clapped alot.

Kari and I watched closely as Rande neared the spectacular finish of juggling three clubs. Suddenly, he tossed one club high in the air, balanced one on another, and caught the first club as it came down. We hoped that someday we'd be able to do that, too.

For his very last trick, Rande juggled a flaming stick in his right hand and three balls in his left hand.

While riding home after the festival, Kari and I talked about all of the new juggling tricks we had seen. We set some new goals for ourselves. Kari wanted to learn to juggle clubs, and I wanted to learn to do some partner work.

On her first few tries, Kari gripped the club too close to its small end. The club flew wildly, sometimes coming near her head. She kept ducking and dropping and laughing, but she kept trying. Rande told her to grip the club closer to its wide part. This is called "**choking up**."

Finally, Kari got the odd-looking cascade going. Then she worked with two pins and one ball. I showed her how to start with two clubs in the right hand and one ball in the left. It took her a few minutes to get used to holding two clubs in one hand, but she soon got it going and was able to practice on her own. Before too long, Kari had managed to juggle all three clubs a few times.

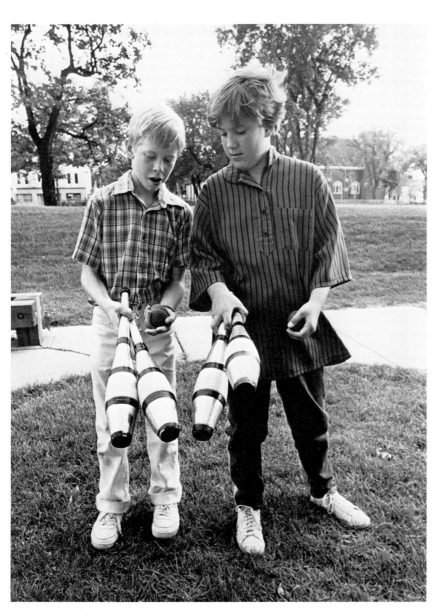

A few days later, Rande and his friend Keith got me started with **partner work**. First, they each juggled three balls while facing each other a few feet apart. Soon they began passing every third ball across the space between them while continuing to juggle the other two.

Then I became Rande's juggling partner. Rande said we would have to start at the same moment and try to stay together, juggling with the same timing. We began with our hands down. Then we raised our right hands, lowered our rights hands together, and started. We each tried to juggle so the balls left our right hands at the same time, and soon we were juggling with the same rhythm.

Rande said to count the throws from the right hand and try to pass on every third throw. He called out, "Self...self...pass," to help me remember. Now it was *my* turn to drop and chase! It took us a long time before we got our first pass to work. Rande said I could practice by facing a wall and bouncing every third ball from my right hand against the wall and into my left hand.

Then Kari and I watched Rande and Keith as they demonstrated other tricks like **take-aways, partner juggling** (or **half-juggling**) and **passing clubs**. The passing looked very fancy as their clubs flashed across the open space.

Rande said that when Kari and I became more experienced, we could also try to juggle other objects. Keith showed us how to juggle cigar boxes, a trick first made famous by comedian W. C. Fields. Rande showed us how to juggle rings and spirit sticks.

Rande wraps his own sticks with strips of leather, but inexpensive wood and plastic sticks are available for the beginner. Rande said working with sticks is lots of fun, because you can create dramatic new looks by varying their speed and by switching between working the sticks horizontally and vertically.

Juggling more than three objects challenges almost every beginner, and Kari and I were no exceptions. We had no idea how to begin. Rande said that in juggling competitions, such as those sponsored yearly by the IJA, as many as 11 objects have been juggled at once! Because of their narrow width, rings are usually used when juggling more than 8 items.

Moving from three objects to four and then to five or more may seem like an impossibility. But Rande assured us that taking it step-by-step and being willing to put in hours of patient practice will lead to success, just as it had for learning the three-ball cascade.

For **four-ball juggling**, Rande started
with two balls in each hand. First, he began
juggling the two balls in his right hand. He
threw the balls from the inside slightly over
toward the outside. Then Rande started the
other two balls in his left hand, again
throwing from the inside. He said this inside-
to-outside technique makes it easier to keep
your hands from getting tangled up.

Rande said for an even more complicated pattern, you can start a left toss just *after* a right toss and alternate the up-and-down movements of your hands. Jugglers practicing advanced four-ball patterns also add cross-overs from left to right. Four-ball jugglers must concentrate especially hard to develop good timing and coordination.

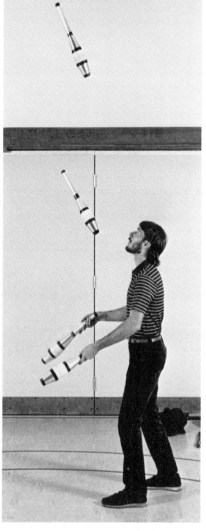

When we were ready to attempt four-ball juggling, Rande told us to first practice juggling two balls in the right hand and then two balls in the left hand. After mastering each hand separately, we would be able to try *both* hands, either together or alternately. He said it would probably take lots of practice before we would be able to keep five, six, or *seven* balls in the air.

Next, Rande juggled four clubs at a time, and then five. Then Keith and Rande passed seven clubs between them!

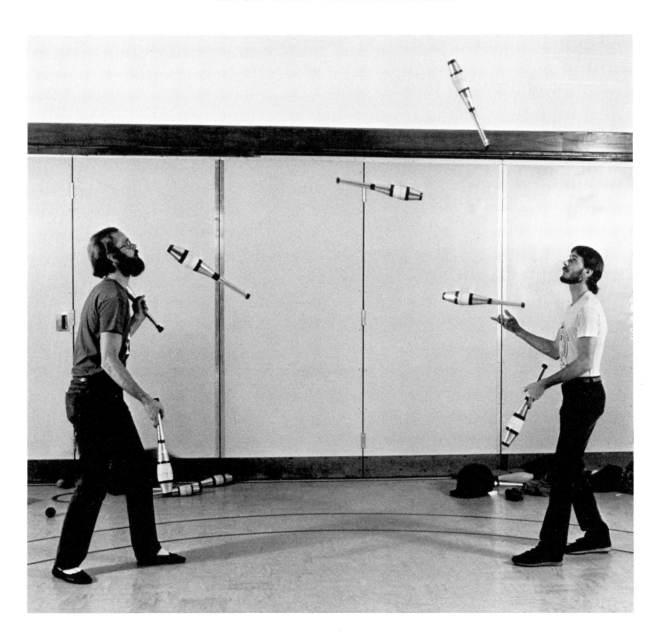

During the rest of the summer, Kari and
I practiced even more, and Rande said we
were both improving in smoothness and
control. We began having contests to see
how long we could juggle without a drop.
One day, Kari suggested it might be fun to
work up a juggling show and present it at
our neighborhood recreation center.

For the next few weeks, we were very busy. We reserved the center for a Saturday afternoon and tacked up flyers announcing our show. We invited our relatives and friends and asked them to tell others to come, too. We planned our tricks, and our mothers helped us sew our costumes.

On the day of the show, we were excited and also a little nervous. Rande reminded us to smile at the audience. At two o'clock sharp, Rande walked out on the stage and introduced us. Our first juggling show had begun!

Kari and I entered from opposite sides of the stage. I was juggling three balls and whistling. Kari, who wasn't juggling, walked toward me, waved, and tried to get my attention. I just continued to juggle and whistle. Finally, Kari stole the balls from me and started juggling them herself.

We loved it when the audience clapped after that first act and cheered for more. Kari juggled with spirit sticks, which she had just learned. I juggled a ball, a ring, and a club. Then I flipped the ring over my head and bowed. For our grand finale, we juggled clubs together, and we ended with a balance trick that Rande had taught us especially for the show.

Performing in our show had been lots of
fun. We are already back at practice—
learning new tricks, polishing our old ones,
and even teaching our friends. Juggling is
a great sport, and it's for us!

Words about JUGGLING

BEANBAGS: Small, pellet- or bean-filled cloth bags used for juggling. Beanbags are especially good for beginning jugglers because they bounce less than balls.

CHOKE UP: In juggling with clubs, to grip the club closer to the wide end than to the narrow end

CLUBS (or PINS): Popular juggling objects, similar in shape to bowling pins, but less heavy

HALF-JUGGLING (or PARTNER JUGGLING): Juggling side-by-side with a partner, with each person using one hand and doing half of the juggling

INTERNATIONAL JUGGLERS ASSOCIATION (IJA): An organization, founded in 1947, that provides meetings, workshops, festivals, and an informal exchange of ideas for jugglers worldwide. For further information, write to: IJA, Box 29, Kenmore, NY 14217.

JUGGLING: Keeping objects in motion in the air by repeatedly tossing and catching them

JUGGLING SIMULATION: To juggle with an assistant. A second person faces the beginner, catches his or her tosses, and places them in the beginner's hands.

LACROSSE BALLS: Balls designed for the sport of lacrosse but also especially good for juggling because of their weight, size (appropriate for jugglers from about age 14 and up), and amount of bounce

ONE-BALL EXCHANGE: A beginning juggling skill in which one ball is tossed up and exchanged back and forth between the left and the right hands

PASSING: A basic juggling skill in which two jugglers exchange one or more of their juggling objects between them while continuing to juggle other objects

PATTER: A practiced speech that a performer gives to his or her audience during a performance

RENAISSANCE: A period in European history (about A.D. 1350-1650) known for a new interest in art, literature, and music as well as the beginning of modern science

SPIRIT (or DEVIL) STICK: A stick, approximately 24 inches (60 cm) long and tapered toward the center, that is popular with modern jugglers. Developed from an ancient oriental toy, the stick is manipulated by two smaller sticks, one held in each hand, and its ends are sometimes set on fire.

TAKEAWAYS: A juggling technique in which one juggler takes away, or "steals," objects from another juggler and begins juggling them

THREE-BALL CASCADE: The juggling of three balls with alternating right- and lefthand tosses. The basic pattern for beginning juggling.

TWO-BALL EXCHANGE: A beginning juggling skill in which two balls are repeatedly passed back and forth between the left and the right hands

WORKING SPACE: In juggling, the rectangular area defined roughly by the juggler's hands and the peak points of the objects being juggled

ABOUT THE AUTHORS

RANDE ARONSON had been juggling for just three years when he won the seven-object juggling competition at the International Jugglers Association (IJA) convention in Cleveland, Ohio. Rande now spends much of his time performing at festivals and special events throughout the United States. He has recently developed a motivational presentation that combines his juggling skills with goal-setting and other techniques for personal achievement.

NANCY MARIE TEMPLE, a former English teacher, spent seven years editing high school textbooks and managing a ballet studio. A recent juggling enthusiast, Nancy now works in Minneapolis, Minnesota, as a children's book editor and freelance writer.

ABOUT THE PHOTOGRAPHERS

BOB AND DIANE WOLFE have a freelance photography business in Minneapolis. Bob studied photography at the Minneapolis College of Art and Design and was senior medical photographer at the University of Minnesota. Diane works as a nursing instructor in St. Paul, Minnesota, and, in addition to her interest in photography, is an accomplished potter.